For the Flowers Never Watered

By Sterling Wilmer

Dedication

Lucky are those whose stories are deemed worthy enough to share
For there are many stories that will never leave the lips of their teller

Never pressed onto paper by pen

Never printed in the pages of a book

Never heard by willing ears

Or received by open hearts

Until now

I will tell their stories

And mine as well

I want to dedicate this work to all the women who helped raise me especially my mother.

I want to thank both of my parents and my family who tirelessly invested everything that

they had to make me the woman that I am today, thank you".

Table of Contents

Chapter 1
We Are All Little Dolls

We Are All Little Dolls

When you enter into a woman

you can't feel her pain.

You can't see the heaviness of the earth

daunting on her.

Her anguish is like a dark shadow

casted over her flowers

named joy and self-confidence.

They haven't been watered in a while.

Nor have they seen the sun.

Yet, you are prepared to fertilize her lotus.

Spraying small delicacies of lust and infatuation.

Don't you really see?

That behind the sensual fragrance

which had you in mid-air floating to her,

are bruises and scars

on the same skin that soaks up that sweet scent.

Don't you see?

 A broken mind

and a torn heart.

The waters of her eyes run so much

that they fill up the tub where she soaks

In mint and lavender oil.

When finally

she gets up,

she wraps herself in lace and bows.

Every night that you come

she is always there to greet you

with a smile on her face

and mango sweet kisses.

Ready for you to enter her,

and distract her soul once more

from the fact that she has lost so much

and gained so little

from the men that come around

just like you do

and knock on her front door.

\-   **Knock and Enter**

I bleed out on the floor

And count the tiny puddles of blood

I was dazed

In and out of conscious I asked why

How?

How did I get to this place?

A black tunnel surrounded me as I zoned into my heartbeat

The sound

It was the loudest instrument in the orchestra of my physiology

And yet I couldn't hear it

All I could hear was a ringing in my ear

And I felt as if I was spinning the room

I levitated

I looked down upon the small and helpless soul

I asked myself

Who is she?

And where did I go?

For the girl that once was

Was there no longer

I waited

I waited for her to fight back

I waited for her to ignite flames and out stretch her charred wings

I waited for her to take a powerful breath into her lungs

to begin to beat the silent drum in her chest

But nothing

Nothing happened

For this is not the girl that I once knew

And so I returned to my chamber

Trapped in darkness

My spirit awaited a reaction from my body

All I could do was still count the tiny puddles of blood on the floor

All I could do was look up

And see

Him

- Come on, get up, and fight

You know

I used to play with dolls

when I was young

But I soon stopped after

Because I too understood how it felt

To be used like a toy

And set aside

Thrown away after they are finished with you

And the excuse was because

They were made of plastic

Well, I am made of flesh and bone

but that still didn't matter to them

Now, did it?

-Childs Play

I still find myself searching for her

The child

The one who did not think of her beauty yet

Or who to compare it to

The one whose imagination gave her highs before drugs ever
touched her cold little hands

I look for her

I reach deep down in the murky swamps of my soul

Just in hopes

I could grab her by a pigtail

And can pull her out of the thick filth

that has pilled on top of her

Suffocated her

For years

The last fresh breath she ever took

was her first inhale outside of the womb

And here I am

Trying to protect her

When it's already too late

I have lost her

-That little girl

I was flying

Through it

In it

Above it

All

I gasp for air

And welcome the fluid into my lungs

Into my nostrils

I have been deceived

For the serenity I once knew

was not true

The weightlessness that I felt

was not due to flight

But due to depth

I was floating

Under it

In it

Through it

All along

And now look at where I am

Simply because I refused to just open my eyes

And see that I was drowning

Before I took a breath

- **Depression**

The best part about life

Is the gift of death

An undisturbed rest

in which no one can break

No annoying alarms or screams

That try to get you to wake

You sleep

Just as tranquil as a full new born

Who just ate

I cannot afford to lose myself

To all of this mess

I am all that my parents have

If I take me

There

Will

Be

Nothing

Here for them

Left

- Contemplating Suicide

Chapter 2

The Lover's First Web

There is no truth to the idea of love

no logic

it cannot be formatted between the margins of good reason
it is quite peculiar in the most familiar way
love continues to juxtapose all positions

Do not get entangled in his web little fly.

For he is the spider,

and you are the food.

This is the way of nature.

This is the way of life.

You won't find love,

in the belly of another.

-Devoured Devotion

I have never seen a black man cry

    until

    you.

    You fight the tears that have escaped

    from the water ducts of your eyes.

    They moisturize your hands

    as you cover your face.

    You are embarrassed,

    so, you waste them,

    by whipping them on your white t-shirts

    or in your pillows.

    Never will you let them fall,

    into the laps

    or the arms

    of others.

    I want to see them.

    I want to see them with your head held up high,

    as they trickle down your cheeks.

    There is so much beauty in you and in your emotion,

it is

unfiltered

and

unappreciated

but

I appreciate it.

I am glad to have seen a black man cry.

It lets me know

that life

hasn't ripped everything out of you

just yet,

because your heart

is still so full

with love,

for you to cry about

something

you've either

 gained

or

lost.

- Forbidden Tears

I know it's not in your nature,

but,

I

could bring

the lover

out of you.

- A Woman's Magic

God

Just make me a butterfly

With silver wings

So that when I land on his windowsill

He will finally see what a wonder I am

What a beauty I am

He will open it up

and let me in

Like he has never done

With his heart

This is the only way

That I can be close

- A Silver Butterfly

I watched him,

how he moved,

how he organized his shoes,

anally.

I looked up at him as I laid on his bare chest.

There was something very familiar,

but nothing like it.

I looked up thinking he wouldn't notice,

big mistake.

Our lips met,

then our hands,

then our hips.

It was magical.

Truly spectacular.

We tumbled around the room

like laundry.

Surfed on the sheets of the bed.

Climbed up the walls of the room,

as we both climaxed,

and he tapped the walls of my womb.

It was the most reckless love I've ever felt.

A slice of pie made of fruit

that man had been forbidden to consume.

His body was tender,

succulent,

and fresh.

Mine was just as ripe,

with juices flowing from my center

as he bit into my breast.

It was nothing short from heaven,

or hell,

being tangled in this heap of a mess.

I couldn't help but sit back and wonder.

How much of his heart do I truly possess?

- **Sensual Contemplations**

I want your time

I want your heart

Neither one

Do you give out

Very often

-Stubborn love

You truly trapped me

And I cannot escape

I am addicted to the pain you inflicted on me

You warned me

And I warned myself

Still, I thought that I could fight the temptation

But I was no match for your loving

No match for your piercing brown eyes

Picking apart every piece of me

No match for your strong arms

Pining me

Throwing me

Lifting me

My helpless body screaming with excitement

On its toes awaiting the next move from you

Yearning for more

As you stir up my insides

Like no other man has done before

My mind and body are detached from each other

I am left satisfied yet confused

How did I let this happen?

Where have you been all my life?

Is this truly love?

Am I being made a fool out of?

It bothers me that I don't know the answers

But the one answer I do know

is true

When you come knocking

And crawling back for more

You know that I'm going to give it up

To you

- The Thrill in Loving You

Every time I leave you

I hope your arms

Open just as wide

for the next time

I return

I need your embrace to be

just as tight

as the time

When you said you loved me

first

I hope a small bit of a smile

cracks on your face

Because I know you never do

Well, I like your smile

I love everything about you

- Light Hearted Hopes

Your name rolls off my tongue

Like fresh sap

Dripping down the sides of a maple tree

How sweet

You forcing it out of me

Over and over again

Like a chant

As if I was worshiping you

I bet you liked it

Having every wind of my breath at your control

My breasts moved up and down

For you

You could silence me

Or

Continue to have me roaring your name

I was here to feed your ego

Ignite a fire in the pit of your belly

That warmed you all the way to your heart

You fell for me

Way long before you fell into me

But how you have truly taken over me is almost

Crippling

The praise that I give you continues to belittle myself

It is not just a name

But a passage way

To the power

To the control

Of my body

- Not just a Name

Empty rings

That no finger could fill

Empty promises

With repercussions that could kill

But with skin so soft

It reminded me of fine silk

And kisses so powerful

I was told that they could heal

I just might accept

All of the lies still

Because deep in the chambers of my heart

I believe this love is

Real

- Denying the Obvious

If I died today,

the last person I'd visit is

you.

I'd enter your dream

during a beautiful scene

where the pink sky

and brown sands

hold hands

with the ocean blue.

I would tell you all of the plans

that I had for us to do.

We would walk the beach

with diamonds and pearls underneath our feet

and breathe in the sweet air

as moist as morning dew.

I would take you to a hidden cave

with a small whirlpool of water

just for us two.

We would sit,

and we would soak,

until the sun tells the moon

that for now

the day is through.

We would sleep on a bed of lavender

amongst the soft sands of the beach,

and when you turn to kiss me goodnight

I would no longer be in your reach.

You would see one star in the night sky,

dancing across the black.

You will wake up

in a cold sweat,

begging,

praying,

wishing,

for my love

to come back.

- **As I leave you**

When is the last time you cared for someone who didn't care for you?

When's the last time you helped someone, who didn't ask you too?

When was the last time you loved unconditionally?

Have you ever loved at all?

How do I know you'll pick up for me, if I do happen to call?

Baby
Darling
Can't you tell?
That I don't take
rejection
very well.

Sugar,
Honey,
Can't you see?
What you did
put a hurtin'
on me.

Chapter 3

Hurt Stops Here

I've witnessed

Some of the world's most courageous women

Crumble

in the strong hands

Of a weak man

Oh how I longed for his seed

I wanted to harvest it

And bear his fruit

I am at the ripe age

To carry

Such a treasured delicacy

If he would have let me

I could graze my hand over the dry dirt

And bring moisture to the rock of earth

I would bury myself in his soil

And a flower garden would appear

I can whisper to the sapling of an oak

And its trunk will grow bigger

Roots will crawl deeper

Branches will out stretch

So that the leaves can bask in the warmth

I will cry you tears into the palm of my hands

And throw them into a trench I dug

And make you a great river

I would push back the sky's cream pillows

And pull the sun nearer

Just to see the golden glow

that bounces off of your radiant skin

I wanted to give you so much more

I wanted to give you life

Health

Strength

Love

But you violated the rules

Of my garden

You took advantage

Of my kindness

And now

Your feet will never again touch the ground

Of my Eden

I don't think I could love him any better,

my heart won't allow it.

The sound of his breathe against the skin of my lips,

the rush I feel when he touches my hips,

it makes my pulse reach to extraordinary heights.

He makes me feel

alive,

but I don't think I could give him another piece

of me.

I don't think I could break him off any more of my crumbled soul.

I see the harness that he has on me,

but I swear,

I'm in control.

Emotions like tidal waves roll

and my patience begins to stir

and our love begins to

wither.

- Failing Love

You cannot drown your sorrows

In liquor

Soon your liver won't allow it

Your actions are screaming louder than your words

I'm fine "help me, help me please"

It's okay to be vulnerable

With me

But you don't think I'm strong enough

To handle your pile of shit

Well baby I have mountains of it

all on my own

So try again

Just look past my smile

And you'll see the painful staples

Holding up the corners of my mouth

To create it

-You are not the only one

I am no longer

your boomerang

One day

You will throw me

way to far

and I won't come back.

Are you happy?

You did it!

I'm just another notch on your belt.

Even though you're the one who did me wrong.

Truthfully, I did it to myself.

How does it feel to loose a love you never had?

It's like a child on the jungle gym

And the first bar that they just can't grab

And so they leap

And they fall

And they try over and over again

It's like playing a game a million times

Even though you know you can never win

It's like dreaming the same dream habitually

So much that you believe of it to be true

But when you wake up from your unconscious state of mind

Nothing has really changed for you

So here I am

Hanging on

Just like

A Child

A Gamer

And a Dreamer do

Truly forgetting

Wow

Such a pity

To cry over someone, you love

But truly never loved you too

-A Lover, the Most Foolish of Them All

I want you to be afraid

I want you to be very afraid

I want you to feel my anger burn

scorching hot like a summer's day

I want you to bow at my feet

Crippled and tongue tied

Paralyzed as you sleep

I want you to dream of my face and beg for mercy

Beg for forgiveness, beg for more

I want you to beg for more glory

I want to smite you with every sharp word that thrashes from my
tongue

I want you to bleed

Bleed out and wade in the drainage from your oppressed and
tattered spirit

I want to look into your eyes and draw out your soul

I want to leave you lifeless

As you once

Did

Me

- Your Turn

Because I knew way better than to do this

I feel stupid

Foolish

Emotionally clueless

Taken advantage of

And useless

For your entertainment was the only purpose of my existence

I was your little puppet, no strings attached

because you are afraid of commitment

How gross of me to be delighted by your fancy

And there I go in my ignorant bliss

I was dumb enough

To think of this of being more than what it was

Yet

Myself is still praying

For this to be more

Than what it is

-Us

The world,

My world,

is literally engulfed in flames

Yet all of my concern is on

You

And Us

And what we will never be

These thoughts are just simply

wasted

energy

I could never go back to them

after being with

him

It just wouldn't be the same

and

It just wouldn't be right

to be thinking about another lover

Night after

Night

-Guilty Conscious

I know I will never see or hear from him again

Oh well

I might as well

just

Fall into oblivion

I am too bitter

and too torn up

to even enjoy loving

another man

One day

I will find some one

that won't make me forget about the rest

But force me to appreciate them

the pain I experienced

The lessons I've learned

Good and bad

Because when have you ever met a soldier

That has a purple heart

But has never been through the trenches of war

They were my ongoing battles with love

and my last and final lover

Will be my reward

For my courageous

And strong pursuit

Towards love and happiness

- The Worst Battle of Them All

One day I woke up

    I stopped asking why I wasn't enough for him

                And began to ask

                    When did I start believing

                    I wasn't enough for myself?

Chapter 4
An End

My mom told me that on Tuesday

all the birds flew away.

They said to her

that they are never coming back

and they are taking the sun with them.

The trees started to drag their feet,

burdened with grief.

Their leaves wilted away

and the water from

lakes, ponds and streams

went into hiding

under the dirt of the earth.

My mother,

picked up the last butterfly

and serenaded it

before its wings lost their vibrant colors,

and fluttered

no more.

"Oh look what we have done

to our home" she said.

"We are next,

this vessel made of dirt

will return to the earth,

as it is rightfully so".

As she crouched down into prayer

I saw her leave,

like the birds.

Brown clay turned into dust

and circled in the wind,

till there was

nothing left.

- My Mother of Nature

No other men

after him

will ever know

about the poems

I write

for

them

Even when our bodies are wrinkled

and our youth has left us.

Memories have run away

swiftly

like thieves in the night.

One day I will look into his familiar brown eyes again

and know,

once more,

the feeling that was lost so many years ago.

The love that life for whatever reason could never allow.

For what it's worth I never stopped fighting for you.

My silent cries and prayers were kept in the journal pages of my
heart.

I never burned them,

I just kept turning to a new page,

because I knew that my story must go on

even though our chapter had ended.

Look at fate,

isn't it the greatest last gift that life could grant us.

One more look at the love that should have been,

the one who was always there,

waiting,

for this

moment

in the end .

-    **Life's Last Laugh**

Out of sight

Out of mind

to you

Far away thoughts

Do you think about me,

Like I think about you?

Probably

Not

-Sad and Wondering

I will throw flowers

Soaked in butter milk

At the feet of you

And your bride

Call me the flower girl

The one who lost all her petals

To a lover who never appreciated

The beauty of a flower

Such as myself

And so here I am

Gathering my sorrows

Soaking them in what joy I have left

Just to throw them at the feet

Of the one who tore them off

In the first place

Do they feel nice under your feet?

Your bride's soft delicate soles

Are caressed by them

Much softer than mine

The soles that are cut up

From walking on pins and needles

Around you

Come

lead her to the altar

My petals are almost gone

And so will I

I cannot stay for this sacred ceremony

One in which

I had dreamt of being a part of one day

Walking on the torn soft petals

Of your ex-lovers

scorned

-a wedding of petals

I helped make that man

Standing in front of you

Loving you

As he is supposed to

He had to practice

On someone

and

Get some of his kinks out

Your welcome

-Bitter and burdened

I am glad it didn't work out

It would have never worked

He wouldn't have been able to withstand

this here hurricane

anyway

My terrible winds

would have blown him over

at the very first gust

I had to free myself from you

I will always continue to try and scrub you off of me

Wash you out of me

Wipe you off my lips

I try to erase you from my thoughts

I know these things will never be successful

When I see you in public my body goes stiff

You added a stain to my already soiled cloth

That tainted my ever so "pure" existence

Right along with the rest of the splotches

That no amount of stain remover could ever lift

Why you treated me like this I have no clue

I didn't deserve it

I just thought you deserved to be loved to

And you tried to warn me

You showed me the real you

I just didn't want to believe that it was true

But for whatever your reasoning was to abandon me

And treat me like I don't exist

I forgave you not because I wanted to

I forgave you because I want to live

- Healing Amidst Distress

Do you even know

Where you are running to

Before you put both feet

On the ground?

You can tell

By the black and blue bruises

On the soles of your feet

That you don't know where you are going

And whom you're running from

And even though it seems like a long race

And you are covering distance

All you have done is run around

Sporadically

In circles

and you will continue to do so

until your heart gives out

Didn't anybody tell you?

That you can't run from your past

Eventually you will have to face it

If you want to enjoy your future

Everyone likes to think

Of roses

As delicate flowers

And

symbols of love
But forget the fact that
to pick one
you may prick yourself
from grabbing at the thorny stem
Love is the same way
A delicacy such as the gift of true love
Most of the time
has a bloody
stickily
start

- A Real Rose

We made it out from the bottom

Of the belly

Of the beast

We crawled out

Through its mouth

By sliding in between

It's teeth

We escaped

It's asphyxiating clutches

As soon as it went to sleep

And now that we are free

And feel like we can finally breathe

The next monster is waiting

around the corner

because what in the hell am, I going to do with this degree?

- College

One day we will all be flowers

dancing under trees

We will bring vibrant colors

to the world around us

And feed the last of the honey bee's

but whenever the soil dries up

We'll know that it's time to leave

Our friends, the butterflies

will spread our seeds

to lands that are in need

of beautiful flowers

dancing under trees

Chapter 5

Beginning

I know it hurts,

I feel it,

seeping deep down

in the most delicate

cracks of your soul.

You were hoping

he could fill them

with eternal joy,

but he was a temporary fix

to a bigger foundational problem.

You've lived through worse,

worse than this heartbreak,

and if you haven't,

then you just haven't lived long enough.

Fix yourself first.

Become the warrior you always

dreamt of being,

because just surviving is no longer enough.

Plan your attacks on love and life.

Rise up above it all.

Come back to yourself and see

that you are much stronger

than all of what tried to break you.

None of this will really matter

when it's all over.

Just keep fighting.

Keep loving.

Keep dreaming.

Keep living.

You will be okay.

-Assurance

One day you will feel my wrath,

and one day you will hear me roar.

The girl that you once knew before

will not be here anymore.

-She is now a Woman

Humans always ask,

why do we hurt?

Did you even think about?

How glass must be shattered sometimes,

into a million pieces

in order to make a mosaic.

Our pain is what makes us

a unique

masterpiece

-Pain with a Purpose

Time is like a terrible two-year-old

Tearing us all apart

But refusing to put us back together

Refusing to clean up the mess that it made

So here we are, collecting the scraps

In an unsuccessful attempt to regather ourselves

After life's biggest tantrums

- **Time The Toddler**

The storm was dark

And unsettling

The rains beat me

Harshly

The pellets

Ripped through my skin

Like bullets

The winds

Picked me up

And spun me

High

Low

Where ever its unforgiving spirit

Decided

I found myself in the aftermath

On the ground

Looking up to the sky

Greeted by a rainbow

I followed it

Because of its promise

It will lead me to higher ground

And fertile soil

So that my roots may once again spread

As I get to the rainbow

I follow it to the end

I look up at its colors

The yellow

The green

The blue

The red

All of them fading now

But when I close my eyes

I can still see them

Vividly

Running across my mind

My soul

Glistens brighter than all of these colors

I am the treasure

At the end

Of the rainbow

- **Hidden Treasure**

Salty

Sweet

And

Savory

lays on her lips

A sensual blessing

but her smirk

was brighter than the light seeping out from the break of dawn.

Her words whistled in the cavities of your inner ear

and the rhythm of her thighs

could be heard from miles away.

Her beauty does not capture,

but it frees.

Her grace is as fluid as the thick oils

she uses to coat her curls.

To do away with all her worries,

the little ones that she has,

she soaks

in a mixture of

mint,

rose

and chamomile

which makes her skin

as golden as fresh honey dripping right off of the hive.

Her spirit does not go unrested for long

and her heavy heart

becomes weightless

with time.

Without a word,

she rearranges the clouds

and encourages

flower buds in the spring to bloom,

just a little bit earlier,

just to see her face.

They are hoping

to be plucked

by her firm and warm grasp.

Her presence in this world

makes all of those

who are given the honor of admiring

such a creation like herself

wish

that they were those flowers,

to be picked,

and woven into a crown

that shall be placed upon her head.

- The Woman with All the Power

If you ever need me

Go outside and look at the sunrise

The crack of light that emerges

Is the slit of my eyelid

Opening to greet you

As you start your day off with early morning meditation

Just close your eyes

You can feel a soft hand brush you in the wind

That is me

pressing on your heart

To make sure it's still beating

And if there is a creek nearby

There will be a current pushing a leaf up stream

That is me telling you to keep pressing on

When I'm gone

I promise you can gaze up at the galaxy

And catch me singing

With the stars as my choir

As I tuck the sun under its covers

Ready for a good night's rest

As you should be as well

Because our day is done

And you must get up tomorrow

Once again, to catch another sunrise

- I am here with you

Color me

vibrantly.

I want you to shade in the lines,

give me depth, and

scribble in my hair.

Illustrate every out of place coil,

smoothly stencil in every single curve and

run your fingers across my markings.

Smudge all the pencil, paint and pastel

into one cohesive piece.

Don't erase a thing,

just admire the beauty,

just admire the mess.

Just appreciate the creative genius who made me.

Gawk at the color brown that the company Crayola will never carry in their 64-color box set.

Bask in the rays of gold, black and bronze that reflect off of my eyes, hair and skin.

Step back and appreciate this wonder.

This masterpiece is called radiance,

and she,

I,

cannot,

will not,

ever be,

remade.

- The art She is

Who needs a husband when nature is my groom?

Who needs a family when you have these beautiful flowers that bloom?

Who needs a church when you and the universe are in tune?

Who needs a house when the earth will never run out of room?

Who needs affection when rain drops kiss your face?

Who needs time because life goes at its own pace?

Who could ever be sad with sweet air tied around you like a lace?

Just take some time to marvel at the earth's beauty

life is not a race

A Prayer to my daughter:

I hope you are nothing like me

I hope you are so much better than me

Stronger than me

Meaner than me

I hope you are 10 times smarter than me

I want you to realize your worth is not dependent on what your body looks like

What's on your face

Or even in between your legs

What really matters is that huge muscle that moves on the left side of your chest

I have made some terrible mistakes, and I want you to make some to

Just nothing that can kill you

I want you to be a fighter

I want you to know how to protect that delicate spirit of yours

I need you to learn how to be selfish

I need you to learn how to love yourself

Even in the hardest times when you really don't want to

Because nobody else will

This world will surely not

Your parents might not even love you the way that you rightfully deserve

And for that I am sorry

I pray that you can master the art of forgiveness for your sake

I pray that you understand the concept of time

and how precious and painstaking it is

Yet how necessary it is for growth

I pray you will never

Never

Love another man nor woman more than you love yourself

I pray that whatever storms blow your way

don't wreck you to smithereens

like they did me

I want you to be happy

I want you to find love

Enjoy friendships

Grow

But I never want you to lose yourself

I want you to feel like you belong

But I pray that you never look to anyone or anything for validation

I need you to understand that the light that is inside you

is enough

That is the reason why you deserve to be here on this earth

It is yours as well as every other human being's right to live

And love

And coexist

Even though the world may say it is not enough

I pray you will not feed into the lies

That the color of your skin

Amount of work you do

The way you believe

Or your passions in life

Solely define you

And in result

Give others the right to put you in a box

Because we don't do straight lines

Exceed all of their expectations

And then set your own

Dance to the beat of your own drum

And then smash that drum and create a new instrument

that the world has never seen before

I hope you are able to explore the beauty of this world

Before we destroy what is left

Take care of the earth

Because you come from it

Most of all I need you to know

You have one mind

One spirit

One body

And one life

Take care of them all!

I want to live

I want to scream my favorite song really loudly in the front seat
of a drop top car

And stick my hands up in the air and feel the wind blow past my
hair

I want to dance all night with a beautiful stranger

No talking

Just moving to the rhythm

Our bodies perfectly synced to the beat and with each other

I want to go to a hole in the wall at 3 am

And eat like it's my last super

I want to terrorize the night

With my beautiful friends

And laugh like there is no tomorrow

I want to feel like a super star

Like I'm the last flower left in a world full of weeds

Like I'm the last fruit tree in a farm full of baron seeds

I won't worry about what the next day might need

Because my heart will stop in this snapshot of bliss

and my soul will never want to leave

-   **A Girl Whose Feet Never
    Touch the Ground**

Men don't make you baby

The lessons that they gave you do

Don't give them anymore credit for

Or control over

A life that you worked so hard to put together

Any fool in the world could have done what they did to you

You are the true hero

Both player

and prize

-To My Sisters

I have hope.

As a single black woman, as survivor, as a loved one, I have hope.

As a student, as a believer, as a lover, I have hope.

I have hope that tomorrow will not be perfect, but at least it will come.

The sun will set, and the moon will rise, and the nighttime will give us rest.

I believe in life and love and the pursuit of happiness without suffering through unreasonable conditions to achieve it.

I have hope that when I hold that little black child's hand and stare into their eyes that I will see visions of them loving themselves unconditionally.

I have hope that when I see a black man upset that he will let the tears flow in frustration, anger or happiness because that is his right.

I have hope for the so called "undesirable" black woman to finally be heard, finally be noticed, and have our existence completely acknowledged and protected.

We all deserve

at least this much.

Everlasting Hopes

She is

Broken

She is

Loved

She is

Praying to the sky's above

She is

Strong

She is

Weak

She is

As pure as a newborn sheep

She is

Lost

She is

Found

She is

Loud without even making a sound

She is

Healing

Changing

Moving

Loosening

She is

Never truly done

I will never let her think again

that

She

is a

no one

-   *I Am Someone*

Chapter 5

Wavelengths

Invisible woman

I remember to move to the side of the street when white people walk by because they still bump into me

I'm the darkest thing walking and they still bump into me

So much room on the sidewalk and they still bump into me

I walk with other white people and they still bump into me as well as them

I walk with black men

and they don't bump into me

Armageddon

If all the black people in the world

Just dared to one day

Open up their mouths

And let out a scream

Let out a cry

Holler from the South America's

To the heart of Africa

Release the breath from your body

Just for 3 seconds

The world would surely crumble

And that is what they have always been afraid of

That is our superpower

Return to Eden:

I hope death is a portal to the lush green paradise that I always deserved.

And I hope I see everyone there that I've loved and lost

I hope they share their fresh fruit with me

And that the nectar is so sweet yet so tangy my taste buds are aroused as the flavors battle for dominance

I hope my lover's are there

And they will message me with the mud and the oils from the earth

I hope my first love is there

Just because I still need the confirmation that some one has ever loved me first

Even in the after life

I hope that I get to see the unborn child that I could not bear to carry

I imagine them slumbering peacefully

wrapped up in large exotic flower petals that bloom when the sunlight needs to hit their skin

I imagine clear streams of water that show the soil and mineral rich bottom

They will lead me to my destinations

And the sky will always be blue

and have clouds in it

And they will give way to a forgiving sun

And a multicolored drawn out sunset

I imagine sitting on a cool rock during a warm night and looking at a sky of beautifully colored stars

And I'll never be tired

And I'll never have to rest

And I'll never feel pain, or sadness, or regret

I hope death is a portal to the lush green paradise that I always deserved.

I hope that I can return to Eden

PARTY GIRL:

When the Sun goes down I love to howl
And the moon rises and I scurry
I run around in circles chasing my tail

And I draw thick eyeliner under my eyes before I leave
And I crack open a bottle of gin
And I paint my lips with the most crimson of reds
Then I line up my leather skirts slit with my outer thigh
And I laugh in the mirror singing to myself
I shout in the darkness wailing at the stars outside of each and every
bar
I take my claws and unforgivingly dig them into a willing victim
And they love it
They love it when I stumble across their feet rushing to make my
way to the bathroom
They love it when I draw my tongue across their skin to see how they
taste
They love it when I scream and bark
They love it when I howl

And when the moon goes down I settle
I snuggle comfortably in my den alone
And I wipe off the eyeliner and the lipstick

I take off the skirt and leave nothing left other than bare fur

I close my eyes and remember what seemed like an endless night of
merriment

I remember all the reasons why I love so much
To howl at the moon
Especially when the stars are out

On the ground where you built

You built on top of the ground where my blood was shed
And you made something beautiful
Something whole
Something positive
And healing
And full of joy
And laughter
And love
Everything
That in that moment I wished I had
You broke ground on where I was was broken
And there is no trace of me left
There was no room for me there
No room for suffering
Pain
Confusion
And secrets
And it's lovely how you planted flowers to bloom in the spring
And trees that would give us piles of leaves in the fall
But the air still smells the same to me
The same as the times when I was so lost
And so young
And I could never imagine you building on top of the ground where
my blood was shed
And making something beautiful from these unknown evils
I tip off my hat to you
You will accomplish many great things
That I never will

A Hurt Woman is True Chaos

I always have dreams that everything I would touch turned to dust
and the ground that I walked on crumbled under me
And the sky poured down small pebbles as rain
And my skin was made of fragile glass that was easily shattered
And when I took a deep breath the air would choke me
And when I looked in the mirror, I saw an empty cavity where my
heart would be
And my eyes were bloodshot from the tears I cried
I don't know why I was crying I just did
And I didn't ask to manifest chaos
It just happens

Forbidden Tears

I have never seen a black man cry
until
you.

You fight the tears that have escaped
from the water ducts of your eyes.
They moisturize your hands
as you cover your face.

You are embarrassed,
so, you waste them,
by whipping them on your white t-shirts
or in your pillows.
Never will you let them fall,
into the laps
or the arms
of others.

I want to see them.

I want to see them with your head held up high,
as they trickle down your cheeks.

There is so much beauty in you and in your emotion,

it is

unfiltered

and

unappreciated

but

I appreciate it.

I am glad to have seen a black man cry.

It lets me know

that life

hasn't ripped everything out of you

just yet,

because your heart

is still so full

with love,

for you to cry about

something

you've either

gained

or

lost.

Blood Rain

They say that blood rain is a mixture of sand or dirt that is captured in the water droplets of the clouds.

It gives the rain a red tint, hence blood rain.

I believe it's the spilled tears of our people finally being released upon the earth from which we came.

Am I wrong to be enraged by the past and present struggles of my people?

Call me mad, angry and black but you could never call me a coward.

You can never call me silent lipped.

You could never call me a traitor.

You may address me as resilient spirit of the land, dancer of the sky or, caresser of the sea.

That is where I belong.

In the places that welcome me as a transformative and transitional being.

Not here, trapped in cages called, bodies, races, factions, titles and faiths.

It is draining me just thinking about it.

Taking it all on, the history, the injustice every joyous occasion and atrocity.

We were not built to suffer and yet, immediately after birth, our bodies start to die.

How lovely.

To know that the black body will die much faster, suffer much longer and work much harder than all of the equally good or bad souls in the world with different colored skin.

I am pretty sure that for every suffering black soul that dies from injustice,

that somewhere in the world,

there is,

a blood rain.

My Mother of Nature

My mom told me that on Tuesday
all the birds flew away.
They said to her
that they are never coming back
and they are taking the sun with them.
The trees started to drag their feet,
burdened with grief.
Their leaves wilted away
and the water from
lakes, ponds and streams
went into hiding
under the dirt of the earth.
My mother,
picked up the last butterfly
and serenaded it
before its wings lost their vibrant colors,
and fluttered
no more.
"Oh look what we have done
to our home" she said.
"We are next,
this vessel made of dirt
will return to the earth,
as it is rightfully so".
As she crouched down into prayer
I saw her leave,
like the birds.
Brown clay turned into dust
and circled in the wind,
till there was
nothing left.

As I leave you

If I died today,
the last person I'd visit is
you.
I'd enter your dream
during a beautiful scene
where the pink sky
and brown sands
hold hands
with the ocean blue.

I would tell you all of the plans
that I had for us to do.
We would walk the beach
with diamonds and pearls underneath our feet
and breathe in the sweet air
as moist as morning dew.

I would take you to a hidden cave
with a small whirlpool of water
just for us two.
We would sit,
and we would soak,

until the sun tells the moon

that for now

the day is through.

We would sleep on a bed of lavender

amongst the soft sands of the beach,

and when you turn to kiss me goodnight

I would no longer be in your reach.

You would see one star in the night sky,

dancing across the black.

You will wake up

in a cold sweat,

begging,

praying,

wishing,

for my love

to come back.

The Black Girl's Journal

I wrote this because I was frustrated. I was frustrated at the world and with myself. I felt silenced, I felt hurt, and I felt invisible. I wanted to scream, I wanted to cry and shout and stomp and throw glass into a brick wall. I wanted to go to sleep. I wanted to curl up in the middle of my bed, as I was tucked into the darkness of a cave that I made out of my covers. I wanted to drift off into a deep long sleep. I was afraid. I was afraid for myself, the ones I loved and the children that one day I may or may not have. I am writing this to a black girl who hears me, who understands me, and I want them to know that I see you. I see what you are going through, and you don't deserve to be ignored. You don't deserve to be silenced.

I understand you may not find any of what I am saying as important right now but trust me when I say, you will need to find your medium. I am urging you to find your voice. I want your creative expression of the written word to be unhindered, but I also want you to be able to confidently and eloquently express how you feel out loud, with your words. It is so important for little black girls to master the skills of both writing and being able to successfully transfer your thoughts into speech with just as much spirit. Yes, I believe you are world changers and that you will be speaking to masses, standing up for what's right and building your own empires but, I also want you to know that writing is fun. Writing is cool and being able to express your emotions and or tell stories without having to move your lips is magical.

The journal is a friend that will always listen to you and will "take your word for it" in the most literal sense. You should write about dreams, goals, likes, dislikes and ideas because everything that you have to say is valuable. There is nothing of yours that is too insignificant to go on piece of paper, even if society tells you otherwise. Sometimes in life we can't find the words to write and that's okay. We can look at the page and cry our tears, or be full of happiness and scribble down "I'm happy" or "I'm lost. I want you to be able to harbor your emotions, write them down and eventually be able to set goals and work through them.

Inarguably some of the greatest social, political, inventive, artistic, and literary minds were black girls that journaled. We follow in the footsteps and behind the written pages of women such as Ida B Wells, Phillis Wheatly, Maya Angelou, Toni Morrison and Michelle Obama. The journal is here to help purge all the undesirable and desirable feelings and promote healing in the most non-destructive way. It is to act as a space that fosters growth, emotional maturity and reflection. Writing has done so much for me that I honestly do not have enough words to describe its impression. My goal is not to convince a slew of prolific New York Times best-selling writers, because I know that the world of literature is not everyone's path, but honestly why not? I just want someplace where black girls can feel heard, unjudged, unharmed and most importantly unbothered.

Signed,

A black girl that journals

Final Remarks

Thank you to the incredible women that I looked up to
of every color
and every size.
Thank you for just reiterating to me
how there is nothing like being
a woman.
Special thanks
to the black women throughout my life
who birthed me,
and taught me how I should love myself.
Even though I didn't always do it,
I appreciate you all
for taking the best qualities in yourselves
and investing them
in
me.
I hope at least a little piece of the person
that I am today
makes you proud,
and know that when you leave this earth
the time spent with
that little black girl
was all worth it.
- I love you all
"By the grace of God, I am what I am..."
1 Corinthians 15:10

Made in the USA
Middletown, DE
03 February 2023

23853079R00046